AIKEN DRUM

PETER SANGER

Aiken Drum

Gaspereau Press Printers & Publishers
Kentville, Nova Scotia
2006

For M.

… expect to write in water and cast in sand.
Palinurus

There was a man lived in the moon, lived
in the moon, lived in the moon,
There was a man lived in the moon
And his name was Aiken Drum.
And he played upon a ladle, a ladle, a ladle,
And he played upon a ladle
And his name was Aiken Drum.
Scottish Traditional

CONTENTS

15   Fossil Fern

16   Snow Fence

17   Listening to Water

18   Geographer

19   Marsh Greens: Burnt Coat Head

21   Newscast

23   Black Rain

24   Windfalls

26   Heidegger, 1933

28   Compass

29   Aiken Drum

31   Medicine Bundle

32   Reader

33   The Fountain

35   Life Mask

36   Cameo

37   Decanter

39   The Earrings

41   Home Economy

43   Renovation

45   Necklace

46   Bookwork

48   A Sensible Horizon

51   Abatos

71   Banbury Cross

76   Walking in Snow

77   After Monteverdi

79   To Clytie

80   The Faithful Huntress

83   Flaught

86   Wind Chimes

88   September Air

90   Chinese Plate

91   Song for Unfolding Silk

92   Three Friends of Summer

93   Rules for the Tones of a Lute

95   Elegy for the Great Auks

97   The Fifth Day

98   Reed Weaver

103   Sable

109   Netkeeper

111   The Mysterious Barricades

112   Firecat

113   The Black Sail

114   Sepulchre

115   Wittgenstein's Circle

116   Moths in March

118   Cana
119   Antiphonal
120   The Loosing
121   The Shards
122   Mozart's Starling

125   Catching Breath: "Abatos" & Others

133   NOTES
137   ACKNOWLEDGEMENTS

FOSSIL FERN

This is the gift of a laminar stain,
an etching of carbon whose
black turns back into green

if you taste it, pinnae
uncoiling, pinnules unfurling
as if they might fly

and flight were one frond away
from this throatful of fern
still growing. A slate of grey

clay is its ground, an earth
you can hold for colour,
shape, speech, all life

in your hands, where spores once
appeared to manipulate silence.

SNOW FENCE

Is this what is meant
by low mimesis,
a fence of red paint
whose slats fit
the same width apart?

Staked out by the road
its successes
survive to be driftless,
except back behind,
drifted.

Wind words thrum through
it such quick
separations of snowflake
from storm. Who
counts them? Not you,

as they fall, as they fall,
and wise
to believe in
unique hexahedron
if ice knows all.

The water waves
back. It goes
with whatever
it is. It is
what it's doing.

It speaks with the tongue
of pebbles, with brittle
clicks of bone,
with shallowing cadence
where gravel recedes

into sand. But these
are not water. They're
no continuous
chambers where nothing
is still and nacreous sound.

GEOGRAPHER

Mapping the world he finds
where we are, a river crammed
into a culvert, a lake concaved
beneath scallions, mountains whose pumice

settled for lowland plain,
shards from an arrowpoint
camp cementing
the strutting container-port.

Cities, towns, farms, drifts
of chosen necessity, desire
preceding intelligence
contract his surveyal:

collator of foxpath,
footpath, transecting midden's
empire. (Still secret their passage,
by word of mouth.)

MARSH GREENS: BURNT COAT HEAD
(*Eleocharis*: Spike Rush)

1. Marsh greens so
    late in the year? Can't
    see why not. With any luck
    his wife will hook her
    a seabass before
    she takes off in the truck
    all tackle and handbag
    to pick a last quart
    of blackberries.

2. Perhaps other
    primitive
    tethers of life
    than
    pinfeather squills
    will pepper your tongue
    with green salt.
    Steam a bit, better
    serve without butter.

3. The man on the mud
gathering greens said
it's mild all around this year.
Something's not right.
The bass don't bite.
Plovers fly rondo
fleet sheer away
overhead, caught
between pick-up and go.

Now that this world has fallen
        into the hands of men
it isn't at all what they want,
        too soft and too hard, too hot,
too cold, too wet. Farce
        up the language. Desert's

fantastically dry, has bugs,
        snakes, scorpions, things.
They bite and make you think
        of the movies, like
the one I saw where soldiers
        were shooting their guns,

and then got mad because they
        ran out of water. Say,
did you see that show last night?
        It had a good shot
of people running away.
        I think they're all crazy,

and afterwards lots of dead birds
        drowning in tides
on the news. What will become
        of it? I've heard some
predict the old man upstairs will soon
        have to close her down,

with wars and these rumours
        of wars. What really matters
is having your health and family
        home to enjoy, especially
at Christmas. I think that the climate
        arranges stuff like that.

Over the edge of the earth another war's
      in progress, covered prime time like ultimate
entertainment. Let us exchange vocabularies,
      inspecting collateral damage long ago
called Death, an old termination whose
      Asian parameters were christened extreme prejudice.

Perhaps we ourselves might mort by unfortunate
      fratricide, though sorties are planned straightforwardly
this way out. Fires stunt the air. Night
      gives a good chance for vision, and heavenly
clouds catch up, gather rain to freight
      in full colour. Oiled opaline, some tears impact.

WINDFALLS

Since I'm too lame to dance I watch
      from an upstairs window
how winter continues at night
      with the old constellations
crossing hands, swinging clear
      as if they could still believe us,

or we them, their modal
      concordance of plow, bow, lyre.
What lyrical arrows can furrow
      our soil. Rockets bloom fire
in sand, need no water,
      and a deer can look out for itself,

ease down across moonlight from hills
      of thickly racked spruce, be there
and be gone as the thin, flat shadow
      which leaps a barbed fence
to leave shovel-shaped tracks that shaft
      under snow after apples.

What planets hang back on the tree?
      If earth, our dear ice, is one,
it sings when you tap like a bowl
      of dry wood and cools
the cold skin on your fingers,
      emptied and equally free.

HEIDEGGER, 1933

(Paul Celan, 1920–1970)

i.   Being inhuman
      cleaves

      humanity's
      being.

      Eyebright
      occluded

      eldertree hangs
      red berries.

      The pilgrim
      will sing
      no, hosanna.

2.   Later
late,
the last singer

struck so
by silence.

Well water
blood, just
a taste.

3.   Dwell on it.

COMPASS

What winnowing
air
hid wind?

Set star
stone by
starlight.

Earth cannot
empty
Elysium.

North? Grow
a calyx
of snow.

AIKEN DRUM

Stand on my shoe
and I'll dance you
around my kitchen.

If, Mr. Moon, you
have cranky ears
I'll play upon

a ladle, I'll play
upon a ladle
and eat cream cheese.

Who ever thought
a razor could
whistle? Willy Wood

did. He died while
attempting. Didn't
have stomach. Spare

are the bones which buckle
it up, earth's longer
garment. We'll all climb

the wooden stair. Write it
in needles, write
it in needles, inside my eye.

MEDICINE BUNDLE

If I could get one, it might look like this,
        bound in white cotton and big
as a book held in bed.

If I could have one, the woman who'd had it
        might guess my sickness
and sign with her chokecherried hands:

You mustn't undo this, or sell it, or give it.
        Hold this on your heart and be well.
While crickets were twittering so-long September

from miles of sunstruck grass, layer by layer
        I'd slowly undo it, peel
cotton and canvas off wool and blank denim,

lift cloths out of pattern, break plaids on their weave
        until I'd uncovered
a cylinder centre of birchbark plugged

neatly by twists of red flannel and tipped
        the piece gently to find
how there's nothing inside.

After a while he got used
to living with pigeons:
plenary courtship, pouterly throb
engaging the sills of four windows,
clerical coos of repletion.

But he had his moments.
His coop fizzled steam. He could
mark the slow morse S
as pressure knocked pipes in the attic.
Such slight declamations

he might at least manage,
and pass on the message, bright
wings battering air,
immutable flumes,
impulsively ultramarine.

THE FOUNTAIN

Remember their year by a story,
how after a summer
of buckets and jugs, they simply
gave up the old well,
an eighteen-foot barrel
of rocks wedged together,
a church without steeple or people
which plumbed at last dry.

Trying to drill a new well
can seem hopeless
as prayer. He guessed that she prayed while
the rig lifted square on flat feet
and bit the first hole in their purse
then mealed through red clay,
grey shale, sluiced by a shot
of pneumatics to spray

wet muck from the bore. But he
wasn't there when a wave
of new water leaped waist high
heaving sand and gravel
prismatic with brilliants of quartz
and following silvery
fountain falling shared grace
in her lyrical voice.

Glossing this episode now,
distant songs of creation.
Or should he depose it as so
unlikely, complacent glissando
where death and sublime resurrection
feast at the sign of the circle?
Pity such choice,
and sacrifice.

LIFE MASK

How else could she act as clown, mime, fool,
as dancer inheriting dance
except by handcasts of shadow
proposing invisible powers? Butterflies
kite fright faces. Moths mimic
leaves, and a toad's dimpled
rubble sips near the tap come dusk.

Over her face, a mask was fitted
from breath to earth. It slept.
It was silent. It woke to be watched through
again. Its speech was a stage
of strange voices, simpler, abstract,
with more love or less
than words he'd already worked out.

The mask spoke them clearly, translating
one version of why he
remembered that time
of miraculous place
when a thrush stopped quiet
cadent falling,
indifferent to light or light.

CAMEO

Nothing at all, with all due respect,
but antique sardonyx, oval
      relievo, pin-clasp intact,

Victorian piece, veined amber.
Quite lovely this hummingbird
      carved at a flower

funnel-shaped, of what to call –
Morning Glory? An ivy-leaved
      not much at all

twined on translucence
concaved to convex by someone's
      incredible patience

as if light itself were the subject,
and commonplace now, unless you insist
      love made it.

DECANTER

You'll never by able to catch it off
        balance. Believe me, I've tried,
and, even in darkness, felt how its weight
        dragged me into a plummet,
pendular, centred, stored, true to just
        one point of rest.

Eclectic Canadian art, Corinthian
        Gothic. But look how it
answers light with starbursts of willow-leaved
        petal looped by elliptical
swags to a quadrupled ravel
        of Solomon's Seal.

Now when our table's set, it manages
        such illustration, and you
accept gifts you've given. Suppose someone
        else believes that earth may pour
out the sky, or that tumblers hold more
        than illusions of water.

There are times when walking from window
        to table means taking life
in our hands, offering, receiving, transforming
        lustres imposed in-between.
Light carved in light gives light back again.
        A crystal's clear stone.

THE EARRINGS

Look at them this way:
you always could hear
much more than any

one else I've met.
Listen, you've said,
and inside your night

are crickets, frogs,
mice whistling solo
between the walls, all goings

on that I'm unable
to trace in my own
unquotable

deafness. We live by empirical
sounds, like those which make
Latin, a little old puzzle

whose pieces must
parse together
or else even simplest

things become at last
incommunicate. These earrings,
as instance, are *diamond*, Sanskrit

for *luminous being*, conjunction
of sun and moon
where words might begin

to yield lightly again
some sense
of the given.

HOME ECONOMY

We've almost built
this room of light

unanchored for now,
adrift and too new

for us to be sure
where even our

pictures have to be
hung. Let's say we're at sea

like the carpet, so blue
you wish we could do

upholstery all over again,
pulling walls down

painting a white levitation
whose aspiration

is air: fact
has flipped off the tailgate

though we've both seen
an iced empyrean

enough and welcome
earth. Light does seem

to remember, domestic
with care, lucific.

RENOVATION

To live in a house
of white gables
with pinnacles flying

bespeaks a particular style:
six walls to the wind
and a wind

that prevails on all quarters
build place we've chosen
to live. Your garden

keeps growing around us
although it's so far
through November we don't

really care about frost.
I wish I could give you
that turn on high

C in Allegri, but you've
given it me leaving
only small words

I can say while we
listen alone and wind
sings the pinnacled darkness.

NECKLACE

Mocking, demanding continuous
miracle, makes little difference

in towers where gold is spun.
Strands which turn while they turn,

coils woven under or
over in constant ravels of either

still plait their helical
concourse, whatever we will.

Doubled, they're one.
Once upon time after Eden,

when earth was the centre,
sun wheeled its circle

above as if light could be left,
and our eyes still glisten ingeminate.

BOOKWORK

First page, first pull, first proof, still the form
dances. Of worries a printer can
never have end. Walk through a press room

when the house has sufficient business
to run all the presses within it –
and still driving books to market

takes a stick to prod and a string
tied fast to the shank of each colophon.
Only printers might see the beauty

of bedsteads in hedges, of a twisted
bicycle stuck in a village pond.
A Heidelberg's all the Heidegger

most of them want, and the sound
of cylinders purling around,
a concord of noise, discordant

to ears unaccustomed to work done well,
with love, suffering long,
without envy or vaunt,

its mystery the grace
of mastery, whenever the hand can find it,
among the music of presses.

A SENSIBLE HORIZON

(*Elizabeth Bishop, 1911–1979*)

The sensible horizon is that circle of the heavens whose plane touches the earth at the spectator.
— Bowditch

Her friend rang up from Florida
as if she might be here,
escaping the death which fetches us
together by flying back
to late imperial Canada.

Alike to her I trust the relative
where secrets can be told,
Boomer, Bulmer, Bowers, spyglass
eyeglass Hutchinsons
who gather and divide

those things which are and those which had
to be. Inside the double
rivers of a dream she saw that
accurate tautology split
through her rooted heart

and carry racing images,
flumes that shut
inside themselves consummate
reflection, continuing
insistently as art.

Which family really was her own?
North turned to south
the farther north she went. I think
of where she said she should
be buried, some four miles south

of a house she often visited,
some seventy north miles,
one watershed away from obvious
Great Village, the old, abandoned
graveyard at The Falls

where frost is breaking every marker
into alphabet, and the shallow
river cutting down one side
flutters white capes of ice
three seasons of the year.

I've also watched such rivers flowing,
depthlessly purged of static
recollection, expulsing all but light,
resolved like her to one uncertain element,
chillingly dark, anciently unfree.

ABATOS

1. Some time in the month
    of July 1812 he turned
    up in Nova Scotia at the prosperous
    port of Windsor. He pretended

    he'd come quite lately from England.
    When asked for his occupation
    he answered, tailor, but
    could turn his hand

    to any mechanical business
    or country employment. Genteel,
    prepossessed, he seemed
    to know himself well.

2.   Finding no better, he entered
the service of Mr. Bond,
a respectable farmer of Rawdon,
conducting himself with most

industrious propriety,
attending morning and evening prayer
with marked regularity.
Bond's daughter applied

to marry him, and so it was done
in 1813, her name having been
Elizabeth P. With her he resided in Windsor
as Frederick H. More.

3.   From thence he worked as tailor
       and peddler together, often
       visiting Halifax, staying overnight.
       That city was plagued about then

       by thefts so numerous
       they were mysterious,
       articles of plate purloined
       from elegant houses, watches

       missing from silversmiths' shops,
       a superior coat caught
       gracing the back of a Windsor
       gentleman, to whom More had sold it.

4.   A warrant was issued. But More
     had escaped on horseback bearing a shark-
     skin portmanteau stocked with desirable
     objects he was able to proffer

     for sale on his way to New Brunswick.
     Once there, in a bye-place
     a mile from Saint John, he took
     quiet lodging as Henry More Smith,

     formed a circle of friendship
     amusing the Ninety-ninth, whose officers
     saw in him something of military character,
     well-acquainted with horsemanship.

5.   Let the brave Ninety-ninth rejoice
      for Smith has perceived the mismatched
      pair its Colonel must drive in his carriage.
      Smith has a better choice.

      Advanced fifteen pounds, he'll secure
      that black horse near Amherst
      he's seen in a field during summer.
      To this the Colonel consented.

      Smith took the money, stole Major King's
      saddle and bridle, then Mr. Knox's horse
      from the field, and rode three days sixty leagues
      before apprehension in Pictou.

6.   At Kingston, a jail between rivers,
where the salt of the lower Saint John
meets the iron of Kennebecasis,
I enter anti-asphyxis.

Am I you, I, Smith (Henry More),
Frederick H. More, Newman (William),
or all the selected Henrys (Bond, Preston or
Hopkins) each a name

given by ultimate Smith
who spoke at a confounding moment
as Henry J. Moon, moonman, moonsmith?
I can't take history for life.

7.   Of middling stature, slender, active,
sick or well, silent, loquacious,
can fence, box, fight, run, is grave
or joyous, can whistle or talk

as occasion suits, amuses himself in prison
by making a puppet show, having
a piece of old horseshoe whetted
on wall as only instrument of mechanism.

He attempts escape by sawing a hole
in the prison door. Through said door
he thrusts his hand, wrenches padlocks,
tries shoving bolts back at the supper hour.

8. God made man out of dust of earth,
    I must make man from wood.
    Caught, I am caught so that
    all I've stolen may turn into gold.

    Spring's not in the offing, that old
    alder business of danglers and cones.
    I'll ride a cock-horse
    through the world.

    There are chains, chains, a collar
    of iron, staples which hold
    me to wall and floor.
    My will can only be naked.

9.   Ariel speaks, fabular
      and antique as a boat-tailed
      autogyro. What manner
      of man is this?

      What manner? I hear
      the waterfall falling,
      word of the waterfall
      falling. What manner

      of man is this? I know
      a language of horses.
      Move gently. Praise softly: Abatos,
      inaccessible, plunging from Pluto.

10.   As a thief, I'm out after justice
not truth. Pull, pull, pull
it all down, presumptuous piety,
pre-emptive pity. I ride the cock-horse.

This is the size of my cell.
Twenty-two feet by sixteen is better
than six. I once pretended to die
and, lo, I was well.

Inside is space for many a voice,
yours among them. Moon
is our nearest relation. He
remembers old mythologies.

11.　　I'm in this for life, a capital
matter. Who would have thought
that stealing a horse could undo
so many? Admit I'm a tangle

of gods. I'll give you fair share.
Look how I've shaped them: puppets
of splinters, with rags
I've stripped myself of to wear,

straw flesh plucked from the tick
of my bed, as if I were thinning
creation. Look how they dance
to my fife, immortal their kick.

12. My hair shall not be shorn
    nor nails cut till I
    grow Sampson-strong
    and then be revenged on my enemy.

    Darkness, darkness, O darkness,
    no light to read the Word
    of God, no word of comfort
    from any. All is

    you rogue, you thief, you villain
    who deserve to be hanged,
    no pity or consolation,
    all trouble, all darkness, O God.

13. On his legs, a pair of steel
    fetters, case-hardened, ten
    inches long, with a chain
    from the middle

    seven feet long stapled
    into the floor. On his neck
    an iron collar with hinge
    and clasp, grappled

    by chain and padlock. Of iron
    there was forty-six pounds.
    Tormenters of man, tear up this place,
    turn it upside down.

14.   Silent, I'll act the fool without
       betraying emotion.
       Let the jury return its verdict:
       the prisoner stands mute

       by God's visitation. If you
       seem to be wise, become
       like a fool. Be wise.
       I'll never speak unto.

       When my irons are replaced
       I receive them as ox
       his yoke, horse his harness,
       escaping, finally sentenced.

15.   Iron I can twist like leather
and break into pieces. I'll use
my own blood for colour, and coal
from a piece of burnt timber.

Dr. Blunt plays a tambourine,
strikes it two or three times.
The lady who swings has music.
Moon whistles a tune.

Henry J. Moon. His Hims. Of Watts
and his Spiritual Songs I'm unable,
brethren, to speak.
I'm a man who makes puppets.

16.   Women, horses, war, power,
       a boy and a girl on the board
       of a teeter, I make them all now
       as if I lived still in a cell of paper:

       the lady who swings, her
       gallant in graceful posture
       dancing, and Bonaparte, cheeks
       red, teeth set in order.

       One of his hands beats the time
       of my music, the other is
       holding my child. I permit
       him a harlequin's costume.

17. I'll ship myself back on the waters.
    Creatures have come about me,
    hogs, horses, all kinds of cattle,
    toads, frogs, snakes – adders.

    Crickets can sing and play
    with children. My sister
    has told me I must not
    hurt them. They cannot pray

    for themselves. I can write
    any hand as handsome or ill
    as you ever saw. I could not
    obtain your question, so left.

18. Pardoned. Why? Sanity,
     madness? A left-handed thief
     has been forgiven. All the crimes
     I'll commit can only be ordinary.

     Accept occupations which need
     a new wearer of clothes.
     God made man from dust of earth:
     I couldn't make man from wood.

     Everything rhymes. Charity
     starts in that fiction. A priest
     prays me out. The jailer opens
     my door: Wholesaler, ash and carry.

19. A man without conscience?
    You are my conscience.
    I've only kept speech
    in a foreign land.

    Rank me the last before you,
    the final forerunner.
    I'm nothing but ever
    appearance and cannot be one.

    Adam Kadmon or
    advocate devil,
    I've ridden a lance
    into Eve's apple, and smiled.

20.   *Incipit parodia.* My name
        is Mercurius Moon.
        I'll speak in any four
        tongues. A tailor

        cuts his own cloth
        upon coming back
        from morning walks on the ocean.
        We're not a terminal myth.

        Death, I pretended to lie
        and was highly successful.
        If I be a tangle of gods,
        believe one could die.

BANBURY CROSS

I.   I rode a mare
      who had three heads,
      one quick, two dead,
      a wish had rode
      the living head.

      Two ways I whipped
      the triple mare
      to separate
      a greening maze.
      We pitched

      us down in shattered wood
      and with her double
      head's shut gaze
      I walled each eye
      that I might die.

The living head
ran on, ran on.
I heard her mane
assume a leaf.
I heard her breath

inhabit water
stirruped
for the sacred fool
I had to give
my death to be.

2. My hands were birds
which flew before me,

my sleeve, the river
they fed above.

At the end of my wrist
one perched singing,

walk you down
by the limber willow

where a wife waits
your faithful widow

holding a ring
which you must enter

to bear a child
and he your maker.

There I walked
by the limber willow.

The child was a child
of fire.

3.   Watch how wind
      anneals with water.
      I am a child
      drowned to save you.
      I am a cockerel
      bloody with morning.
      I am an end
      to your beginning.
      I am a victim
      betrayed.

      Child we meet
      in warm, green silence.
      Now all sunlight
      patterns our stillness.
      What was our shadow
      floats above us.
      Watch how your fingers
      fuse to my tendon.
      Listen, your voice
      is mine.

WALKING IN SNOW
(Richard Outram, 1930–2005)

Bright day! My pen
smells of balsam.

Juncos dance seeds
from the snow

with a scurry of pedals.
Trust you to see light

that day by the river,
its wavering weave

through lichenous spruce.
What you saw

is not seen. So you said:
work ended.

All the true sounds descended to fetch her back,
     water the first with a dapping
of waves upon pebbles and wind she remembered
     filling through riverside spruce
those seafalls which fell between silence.
     She listened, listened,
heard the gather again into fullness
     and fall while a loon's dark
tremulant echoed itself over water,
     whickering close and away
before she could ask that it stop where it was,
     calling inside her. There
from the spruce, a ratchety burr, a clucking
     of truculent squirrels, elsewhere,
jay clack, heron screik, creak of crow wings
     oaring air, a whistle
of black duck circling the old green skiff
     which puddered slicked Acheron.

And next she could see him, ahead at the prow,
      his voice singing mutely, his hands
plucking notes from strings which vibrated in stillness.
      Wordless for now, she begged that he
listen to all the true sounds descending
      to fetch her back, but he sailed
his ceiling of water, his face looking up at his face
      drawing breath with the mouth
of things, and he couldn't just then turn to hear her.

TO CLYTIE

Truly in love with music's close
you're bisque atop the pedestal
of one sweet song by Thomas Moore.
Believe me ... those endearing young charms
affect me still, although your *fairy gifts*
are not the *dear ruin* a poet hoped
he'd cherish later *verdantly*. I *blame not
the bard*. Perennial grief still becomes you,
and alabaster eyes of downcast pensiveness.
You've watched a chariot bounce
on crippled rims, Apollo rocket
to the moon and most forget
your minor myth of envy and betrayal.
Ovid is out, and the priceless transformations.
Which of us cares you tattled on your sister
until she pushed up frankincense, and the god
who'd had you both betook himself
to a pantheon? Such things could happen,
happen now, as you reach from the soil,
part red, part white, beshadowed blue,
turning your flowers towards the turning sun,
loosely attired and loyal valerian.

No, not just a portrait, but also
        a conversation piece,
Ramsay's *Victoria Kynaston*
        painted four years
since the clans were scythed at Culloden
and Hanovers ledgered the wheat.

Indigo, the Virgin's colour,
        her gown is presented
to drape from a backboned armature,
        décolletage framed
by nice calculations of lace:
traditions which lack real self-consciousness

only repeat the present. Hers
        are the past
redeeming the future, offering
        as much to the general
gaze as she considers appropriate,
covert, in fact, to the quick.

Her right hand, held open, extends
    on her lap, second
finger and thumb touched
    in the classical gesture, *indico*,
while the left hand, *silentium postulo*,
fondles the head of a fawn-and-white

greyhound nuzzling lace on her sleeve.
    Must I, like her dog,
hunt by sight? Believing is
    other than seeing: I might
understand when my fingers
turn into feet, my arms

into spindleshanks and no kind
    of speech from lips
can pass. Actaeon falls
    as Artemis gives cry,
and a voice of more tempered persuasion
joined shapes attentively chosen

to fit on a *bit of ivory two inches*
      wide worked
with a brush so fine … to produce
      little effect after much
labour. It speaks with ironic decorum,
a body secure, within right keeping.

FLAUGHT

I knew a carpenter once
        who stood with a fistful
of spikes, held up and ready to pound
        when lightning fizzed
from their tips. He was
        somewhat surprised.

But I'm thinking of Giorgione's
        Tempesta and things
riven by golden thread
        as ironwood splits,
of a spiralling torque through clouds
        of grey wineskin.

Flaught, flight, lightning's
        third light between
night and day. A late adolescent
        in doublet, shorts, lavender
skivvies who leans on a pensive
        staff (there's a ruin
of columns behind him) stares
        across his left shoulder

and over a trickle of brook
        at a naked young woman
who sits on the grass suckling
        her child. This
picture exists for itself ... points the way
        to complete abolition
of subject in all contemporary
        art, or so we may read,

if we care to be timely.
        Beneath the young man
x-rays uncover a cancel
        of pentimento,
another young woman stripped
        to enter the brook,
as though life overlay speculation
        with paint,

as though leaning Narcissus,
     rapt in a glance
of posed attachment, were always
     his own second thought,
unaware of another existence,
     of the child who suckles,
of the woman who watches
     none but us.

WIND CHIMES

Wind chimes awake the garden
with pebbles of water. A song sparrow
sings, singly for doubles to learn.

From life to love
what changing measures ring.

Immortal the dew. Who can
still sleep? July plays away
its night so quickly.

From love to life
an open measure rings.

This time is another, where
trailing arbutus prepares
concealments of mayflower.

From life to love
a hidden message rings.

Light, dark, percussively softly,
night into shadow mantles
the vale, earth's body.

By love and life
all other measures ring.

September light is at rest,
has entered the glass of itself.
As for time, it's transparent.

*From dance to dance the air
of life goes on.*

Blackberries freshen in silence.
Ash berries almost ignite
precise constellations.

*From air to air the dance
of love goes on.*

Nothing else needed,
and words
which vows have renewed …

From life to love the dance
of air goes on.

truth, honour, joy,
heart's gentle consent
to this reverberant day.

With dancing life the air
of love goes on.

CHINESE PLATE

Under its glaze of transient empire
      earth goes on as before
      colouring summer,
sea, sky a concordant azure.

If a merchant has entered
      your courtyard,
      then butterfly, bird,
seed pod and blossom, gold

gilding green, chrysanthemum pink
      and his silk
      of coralline lilac
assemble the brushwork

of elsewhere. Pure
      is the land wherever
      you are.
As fowls of the air

we might remain human
      and a lute's thirteen
      studs illumine
like stars. The moon continues to listen.

Unlikely we'll live on the dust
        of a pearl;
meanwhile, there is silk and the slow
        unfolding of silk.

If what it reveals is a veil
        at least it is
oxidized lustre, the filatured
        seed and flower,

the flight of a cinnabar bird
        whose wings are lappets
of thread. If stars
        drench indigo night,

if glittering still takes and your
        brave vibration
casts moment to motion
        across the poise

of your hands, then darkness
        becomes the first stage
of shadow, as light
        is the last.

Three friends of summer
agreed to meet in a garden.
The less said the better.

It once was sufficient
to name their names
to know why they met.

Plum, pine, bamboo gave brilliance
with shadow while wind raised
each separate susurrus.

Cones on the plum had spoken
corollas of pollen. Bamboo tripped
a clicket of trickle gates open.

Pine built a terrace
of boughs overhead, overheard
as dissilient silence.

Three friends once met in a garden.
Their talk concerned earth,
concerned heaven, the human.

Messenger of lovers, sigh carrier,
its tones are governed by clearness
as left hand and right chant together.

They depend upon touch. Consider
a string thin as a single
silk thread, a sound

marred when fingers approach too quickly.
The slow touch is base to the swift,
the swift an echo of slow,

light but not floating, swift but
not hurried, flowing not stet,
crescendos and de-crescendos

crisply connected. Ride upon horseback
among white clouds. Strike bronze bells.
Two cinnabar pendants chime in a passage

from garden to gate. Suggestion
never describes. Flowers speak with flowers.
To indicate does not define.

For the strings
of the heart have their own nature,
empty the step which treads upon air.

Did some of them wonder if we
were a version of them, equally
flightless and granted to stand
like a refugee crowd
in the square of some levelled city?

Like ours, the carcass was fat
and could reputedly feed
the fires which rendered it
down into purest
oil, hotly as driftwood.

I've read they were docile.
They'd herd up gangplanks, waddle
abreast, and placably queue
awaiting our execution.
One might say, from the utile

view, there is little reason
to mourn their destruction,
though fresh or in salt they
made us provision aplenty
and still might have done.

In this best of all possible worlds,
dolphining douce
underwater, did they sense
small bones in each wing
pulling forward like fingers?

But they never left their gods.

THE FIFTH DAY

1.   Released into shadow, I saw
    three horses of darkness, the roan,
    the black, the bay, grazing
    a field by the river and smelled
    their leathery barm.

    Small night had fallen away,
    a greater stayed. They trod
    green alms of a dream, slowly,
    more slowly, in the place of the flail,
    where oxen trammel wheat.

2.   Let them lie if you must,
    but one I saw once
    when I slept, a red-and-white
    spaniel whose rocking-horse prance
    chased the white stag of the world,

    antlers racked back in a gyroscope's
    trim, pursued, pursuing pursuit,
    a chase caught by chase with no
    beast in view. Wars were
    unfought. Lovers held true.

REED WEAVER

When I telephoned to ask, his daughter
        said he was dying, but
she would see. At least, perhaps he might
        be interested, and please
could I call again, a day or so
        later. Who really spoke
persuasively? She, or the claw of the crab
        and the need to do just one
more time what he'd apprenticed to learn
        in Holland, back before the war,
when the job you started learning at fifteen
        was the job which saw you
out? His was caning, cording and weaving
        seats for chairs.

I had two chairs worth doing, pillow-backs,
        each with a grecian urn
in mid-slat, fretwork silhouette,
        a pair of country-
Chippendales, carpentered two centuries ago
        ten miles up the road.
I'd salvaged them seatless, partly broken,
        at a yard-sale barn
where seven cords of seasoned furnace wood
        offered a far more
sensible deal. *Bring me just one*, he said, *I'll see*
        what I can do. It was spring.
You'll have to wait till reeds grow long
        enough by the river.

One chair I brought and listened while he
        told me something of what was
more and more in his memory,
        of how he'd come to Nova Scotia
forty years before and made a living farming
        or, more like, lost a living,
making it up by odd jobs labouring and cutting
        pulp; and while we
spoke I felt the draw of another tongue,
        not Dutch so much, though
that was partly so, but more a language
        he'd had to learn that said
how to carry his hands and newly lay them
        down, if he was to survive.

Some six weeks after, in July, his daughter
        phoned to say I should
revisit, bringing the second chair.
        Beside the fireplace which he'd
built right after he'd retired was the first
        with a seat of woven reeds,
cylindrical cords he'd trimmed and ravelled round
        then laced into four
equilateral triangles whose apices met
        at centre point to make
a square. He'd placed it on display to show
        his friends what I called
beautiful and he called what you could
        do with reeds.

By middle August both the chairs were ready.
      How much did he want?
Enough to be sign a fair job was worth
      his fairly doing. Too little
as sign maybe I'd listened. When I brought
      the pair home their reeds were
green and filled the room where I set them
      with a smell of freshly
baled hay in the mow and the sun at work,
      greening, still growing
it seemed. Grains of green light inflected
      the cords as if ancient
faith, present courage, continued. That autumn
      he died.

SABLE

Even before you begin to remember
      I imperceptibly shift.
I'm fluent as water carving from sea
      a travelling harbour of sand.
I conjure horses of night to run
      forth by day. I trace
what the many-voiced sing: salt
      and the sea-green bronze
where sea has cast it; this cat's-paw
      flurry, one breath below
land; and taller the horses at evening
      dancing on stilts of shadow.

Flat clang of a bell off Cape Misenum,
        what's that to me? No
antennary art. Pick a quarrel
        with Triton, you'll get
the triple harpoon. All I know is this steeple,
        this shuttlecock bob
of red steel which shudders in chains
        towards me, even at neap,
as if that were freedom and I an isle
        without way, in the way
of its flat clanging bell, tolling arrhythmic,
        unpredictably struck.

Palinurus? He perished by sleep despite
      drumheaded wind.
Like mine were his eyelids. Fate threw the weight
      of their coins.
Dark, I still sing, turn sunwise to mill
      my own whetstone with all
the time in this world. When north side and south
      have met I'll
slither the slope of my mountain
      back down into ocean.
His requiem now? Cast a brief oar.
      Scatter dust into water.

Sable, I'm white and black, black as heraldic,
      white as the sand I carry.
I'm mourning and morning. I'm skin of the world,
      cut, peeled, stripped, then rubbed
styptic by salt. I'm pegged out to dry.
      I'm silicate life
caught between crystals, convergent with currents
      of wind, tide, language, light,
an imaginal island no man can touch,
      taste, see, smell, and hear
when I'm cast into sand at that moment
      voice fills the air.

I propose intermediate passage.
      One hook of sand is leash
to the spineless dogfish. I hid the house
      where two lovers met
beneath perfections of gravity. Its shingles
      were buffed sparrow silver.
Swallower of ships, wreck seiner, collector
      of tubs, drums, jugs, bottles,
by the end I'll have gathered all the lost
      manufactures, a float
of green glass in which will be wordlessly
      found my world without me.

Do you know this land? It lies between earth and sea.
My grave is unquiet.
It needs the green tree. Or is marram
laurel enough, and the single day's
bloom of dog rose? I offer the shadow of horses
and a silver grey sparrow
whose song is both close and secretly distant.
It begins with a lisp
of dry grass upon driftwood. It ends with three
notes diatonically angled,
obliquely away. Leaving as migrant,
it carries itself almost silent.

NETKEEPER

A punt of dubbed leather, material fact,
        as the ball in exact
parabola strikes where I've chosen to stand
        and tosses towards me in bounds
a catch off-spin which calibrates through
        before I can see it. Are
meshes fraying apart, or do they square

wider as light turns older? Must we catch
        the ball of ourselves flying outward
and let it fall? Nothing I name and sing
        and never dispel divides me
from some climbing lob and the need
        to catch or be caught. Are we net,
sieve, last noose of nothing, knot

by which nothing takes form
        when the ball approaching the ball
approaching the ball slows to eleatic
        arithmetic where nothing
is substance, abiding in motionless
        motion, not
nothing itself? Infinitude finite,

bail of the sun, ropes which strum whenever
      dew slackens, sifter of shadow
whose form can only be light, tell me to leave,
      I'll leave. If gods did betray,
I also betrayed the gods.
      No need to call the game over.
Catch as catch can. The net continues secure

as once on a summer I caught and carried
      in green glitterfoil
a hummingbird's measure of pulse
      and breath from the pane
where it stuttered away and opened
      my hand to the flight of its world,
vanished, unhesitant, uttered.

THE MYSTERIOUS BARRICADES

(François Couperin, 1668–1733)

Sound a full chord. Extend the notes
  over time. Connect, enliven,
elucidate music by touch, shakes,
  quavers, trills, cadences full
or broken and still it must reach
  return, the theme carried through
at the turning, the clef
  of not what has been
but what happens again and again,
  some infinite moment.
Wherever you go, you meet yourself
  leaving. You hear
an angel of sand. She speaks
  a minute particular.
Are you there? And echo replies,
  you are there.

FIRECAT

Track of a firecat
fresh in falling snow
and I quickly carried
its skull as a socket

for eyes, a harrow
of teeth curved
like tubular sabres
when iris blow

back towards spring. A bullet
projected so slowly
I watched while it entered
the skull, split it

liquidly open, scattered
flame and the firecat
was human, seemed
lynx with leopardine head

saying *I am not dreamed.*
Kill me. I'll never be dead.

THE BLACK SAIL

Eros unknown, god of descendant forms
        ascending, was it you
I saw once in your pride, there in the blood-red
        room where heartbeats
        pulsed each wall?

I watched as you smiled, and the smile
        was so old it curved
itself into stone, re-curving as flesh
        freely held
        while you gestured

across to a window widening
        unglazed open, unsealing
the air below where a city, sea-girt,
        lime-white, instantly
        terraced itself

from blue water. How shall a city
        be wise without unknowing?
How shall it stand? From our height
        the ship still returns,
        black sail unfurling.

Let them walk through the orchard amazed
by apples, some keepers, some spoilers.
Let them call for the gardener, already
in Eden, who grafts with parable shears.

Let them find the great stone pushed back
and then, stooping down, looking
in, see scattered scraps of white linen,
an ultimate plenitude. Nothing.

Shouting instructions, becoming breathless,
    Wittgenstein danced
on Midsummer Common what was to hand
    of this solar system,
himself, his disciple, whose wife
    was the sun and steadily
paced the meadow, while Malcolm
    (disciple) as (earth)
circled her at a trot, and Wittgenstein
    ran round him the moon's
    tight dizzy of circles.

Is there nothing of grief but mind? A viol's
    slow bow draws voice
at the tuned edge of things. Serving mystery
    with no mythology
but the myth of an absent god, he wrote
    . . . riddle does not
exist. To grieve in private, continuing public,
    was never an art he lost.
Arrange what you've almost known.
    He'd close his eyes,
    troll pennies for prizes.

MOTHS IN MARCH

Tricornes of paper,
improvised tabs torn
from notebook pages,

mid-month, come thaw,
they appear, either wise
or projected by

wisdom so small
it mistakes
the March sun

at midnight
for midsummer's
moon. Nuptial to nothing,

living for less than
one night, they absolve
as silvery ash,

flicker out
like oil lamps
on Patmos.

No wall of no
house can stay their
invisible storm.

CANA

Nox nocti. Night, darker night,
and I hear the river
levelling in leaf after tide
has brimmed its spate.

Drink from this cup of sand.
In earth's deep jar, wine turns
back into water. So you might
weep. Or make my voice glad.

ANTIPHONAL

Praise those which bloom
before they breathe into leaf,
daphne, magnolia, plum

or her arising from *tabitha*
cumi, a child still asleep,
sharp cherry and yellow forsythia.

THE LOOSING

What will you do, little black horse,
when loom weights unknot their thread,
when tric-a-trac hammers

down in the coppersmiths' quarter are still,
when cutlers must sharpen blades with rust
and cups of a potter can only spill

air? Little black horse, will you think
of the last of your riders leaning
lightly upon you to thank?

THE SHARDS

Shatter a box of nard
to pour on paradise field.

Crush a white strophe
of alabaster. Given, give

all in full measure. Break,
and Judas will speak.

MOZART'S STARLING

Sing in your cage
as if nature and art
were one. The age

is seldom propitious and you,
little fool, despite your brag,
must whistle through

fire and water, allegretto
as we, a theme
from the G major concerto

written five weeks before
he'd ever heard you. Pa-Pa-
geno, I mean, birdcatcher

and bellman, with one year
to live while music
and love endure.

"Abatos" is based upon a book as bibliographically elusive as the biography of its protagonist. The book originally appeared in what seem to be three different first editions, bearing three different titles. In 1817, Allman and Co. of London, England, published *A Narrative of the Conduct and Adventures of Henry Frederick Moon, alias William Newman, a Native of Brighthelmstone, Sussex and Now Under Sentence of Imprisonment in Connecticut, North America: Containing an Account of His Unparalleled Artifices, Impostures, Mechanical Ingenuity & C & C Displayed During and Subsequently to His Confinement in One of His Majesty's Prisons.* The same publisher, in the same year, issued the same text with the title *Companion for Caraboo: A Narrative of the Conduct and Adventures of Henry Frederick Moon* … and so on, as above, while in New Haven, Connecticut, also in 1817, Maltby, Goldsmith & Co. published the book as *The Mysterious Stranger, or, alias William Newman, Who Is Now Confined in Simsbury Mines, in Connecticut for the Crime of Burglary: Containing an Account of His Extraordinary Conduct During His Confinement in the Gaol of King's County, Province of New Brunswick, Where He Was Under Sentence of Death: With a Statement of His.*

The overlapping and extravagant activity of these three titles suggests that the publishers sensed opportunity. If so, they were right. The book, whose title I will now trim and stabilize into the one by which it has become generally known – *The Mysterious Stranger* – went through two editions in both London and New Haven in 1817. Since it is set in what became Canada, it should be accounted the first Canadian best-seller. Unlike many such best-sellers, it has gone on to a lively, continuous existence. The printer-publisher W. Cunnabell reissued it in Halifax, Nova Scotia, in 1835. In 1840, the book's author, Walter Bates, according to the title page, "enlarged and improved" his 1817 text, and it was published as the "third edition" by W. L. Avery of Saint John, New Brunswick. This amended edition was reprinted frequently in the Maritimes throughout the rest of the nineteenth century, advertised at times as a fourth, sixth, or seventh edition, although no alterations to Bates's 1840 text occurred. The spirit of Alias-Moon was exceedingly busy. Library and Archives Canada holds copies issued, fairly equal in number, by either J. A. Bowes or G. W. Day, both publishers in Saint John. The copies are dated 1855, 1856, 1857, 1866, 1872, 1878, 1887 and 1895. I doubt whether that list accounts for all the New Brunswick printings, but it is still sufficient to show that Alias-Moon must have been, in New Brunswick at least, one of the infamous figures of the day. My own copy of The Mysterious Stranger, published by Bowes in 1910, is a crumbling, paper-bound, stapled booklet of 168 pages. Like all the examples of the book I have seen, it bears the distress, or comfort marks of having been opened by many hands. After 1910, the book's popularity seems to have lessened, but because it is most likely to be available to a reader of "Abatos" one of the few twentieth-century printings should be noted here. In 1979, 1980 and 1981 (perhaps there were further printings), in Woodstock, New Brunswick, The Mysterious Stranger was published by a company named aptly (given Alias-Moon's exploits) the Non-Entity Press.

The book's author, Walter Bates, was born in what is now Stamford, Connecticut, on March 14, 1770. In 1783 Bates was among the Loyalist farmers living as refugees on Long Island who accepted the Crown's offer of 200 acres of land in Nova Scotia, together with two years' provisions. He arrived in Parrtown (which became Saint John) on the first ship of the 1783 Loyalist evacuation fleet. He settled in Kingston, just north of Saint John, on the peninsula formed by the junction of the Saint John and Kennebecasis rivers. Bates became the sheriff of King's County. He also took a leading part in the founding and building of Trinity Anglican Church in Kingston, where he served as a lay reader. He died on February 11, 1842.

Bates is the author of two other books besides *The Mysterious Stranger*, both completely unlike it. One is an account of his early life in Connecticut, of the 1783 voyage and of the settlement of Kingston. It was not published until 1889. In addition Bates wrote a defence of the Anglican church entitled *A Serious Conference of Letters on the Subject of Religious Worship and the Church of God*, which was published in Saint John in 1826.

The evidence of these two books and of Bates's life as a sheriff and churchman is that he only told what he believed to be the truth. He was no romancer. The apparently unbelievable stories about Alias-Moon in *The Mysterious Stranger* are difficult to dismiss as fabrications – all the more so because

Bates carefully named co-witnesses who were known and respected in Kingston and Saint John. We have two choices: either Bates's account is factual, or Alias-Moon had the ability to transmute illusion into the semblance of reality by the force of his character. Either choice leaves the veracity of Bates's narrative intact.

To insist upon its veracity, however, is not to concede that *The Mysterious Stranger* is without literary antecedents. Every piece of writing has them. They frame the manner of Bates's tale and, I believe, some of his factual emphasis. Two of these antecedents, in particular, are unlikely to occur to modern readers.

The first would have fallen into the category of professional reading for Sheriff Bates. It is *The Malefactor's Register; or, the Newgate and Tyburn Calendar ... from the Year 1700 to Lady-Day 1779*, a multi-volume series of biographies of English criminals, with accounts of their behaviour in prison, their trials and punishments, which began publication in 1773 and continued to appear sporadically in various updated and re-edited versions well into the nineteenth century. It is usually known now as *The Newgate Calendar*. From it, Bates could have learned, first, that there was an avid audience for exploits like those of Alias-Moon, and, second, that it was possible to write the biography of a criminal with, on the writer's part, a judicious mixture of moral disquiet and relishing curiosity.

The second of these literary antecedents is a more subtle one. I believe it is William Godwin's novel *Caleb Williams*.

(Godwin is remembered now mainly for having been the father of Mary Shelley, the author of *Frankenstein*, not published until the year after Bates's book, but having a curious undercurrent of thematic connection with events in Kingston in 1813.) First published in 1792, *Caleb Williams* had achieved four editions by 1816 and was one of the most famous novels of its time. Because of its analysis of the English judicial and penal system, Godwin's novel would, like *The Newgate Calendar*, have interested a man of Bates's occupation. But there is textual evidence to suggest a deeper link between Bates's book and Godwin's.

The most obvious parallel between *The Mysterious Stranger* and *Caleb Williams* is that each protagonist must struggle to free himself from chains and handcuffs while incarcerated in jail by using the same kind of mechanical ingenuity, improvised implements and physical dexterity. Both protagonists break or cut fetters, loosen window-bars, dismantle stone and mortar and attempt to escape detection by means which Godwin and Bates describe in similar lengthy passages of forensic detail.

A less obvious but all the more striking parallel occurs when the protagonist of Godwin's novel, having escaped prison, encounters a peddler selling a broadsheet entitled "The Wonderful and Surprising History of Caleb Williams." In effect, the protagonist, Caleb Williams, has encountered a performance of what he had rehearsed before as himself, a performance which, at one remove beyond the peddler's broadsheet, becomes the novel in which we read of Caleb Williams as protagonist. Similarly Bates's book, especially in the title-page extravagances of its 1817 version, is a performance by Alias-Moon, a performance initially rehearsed while that elusive non-entity was still in the midst of the various names by which Bates knew him. In one more twist, Bates's 1840 revision of the 1817 version attempts to follow his protagonist's later criminal career, first in New England and then in Upper Canada, where a prisoner in the Toronto jail in September, 1836, whom Bates believes to be the mysterious stranger, is confronted with a copy of the 1817 text and asked to identify himself as its subject.

The prisoner refused to do so, but I think Bates was right. The Toronto prisoner was the man, or rather, the many men. He may even have read *Caleb Williams* himself. In fact, perhaps Alias-Moon had acted the part of Godwin's protagonist for Bates, and that accounts for parallels shared by *Caleb Williams* and *The Mysterious Stranger*.

For the protagonists of both books are driven by an imprisoned selfhood we know to be guilty and sense to be innocent. Their aim is escape, but all their efforts to escape become details which lead up to their captures. Both are as much at liberty as Autolycus and yet as much possessed as Iago. They have in their composition the "fatal fantastic element" of post-Enlightenment human beings analyzed by the narrator of Dostoevsky's *Notes from Underground*. In their prison cells, they set themselves the task of dismantling, literally, what Dostoevsky's narrator calls the "stone wall … the laws of nature." Their cells are equivalents to that "abstract and intentional city" St. Petersburg – for Caleb Williams, the malignant squirearchy of pseudo-chivalric Tory England, for Alias-Moon (a.k.a. Newman/new-man), the Anglican kingdom of refugee Kingston, with its sheriff and lay reader Walter Bates. By the end of *The Mysterious Stranger* (1840), in fact, it is equivocal who has been apprehended. A fool's fool is the king.

"Abatos" tries to do justice to such explicit, implicit ambiguities. The sequence of poems has omitted some events, notably Alias-Moon's second escape, and simplified others. At one point, for example, Alias-Moon's company of puppets numbered two dozen rather than the preliminary half dozen with which I have left him, although one of the latter truly was Napoleon. In a few instances, "Abatos" also transposes incidents and speeches from its protagonist's later career into Kingston jail in 1813.

But even when making these changes I was faithful to Alias-Moon's qualities, whether he acted as thief, liar, master mechanic, carnival strongman, puppeteer, escape and escapement artist, schizophrenic overwhelmed by a mercurial archetype or double-dealer with a dual soul. For he is also the inner breath of language, whose power wanes if pardoned.

EPIGRAPHS See Cyril Connolly [Palinurus], *The Unquiet Grave* (New York: Harper & Brothers, 1945), p. 57, and Iona and Peter Opie (eds.), *The Oxford Dictionary of Nursery Rhymes* (Oxford: Oxford UP, 1980), pp. 52–54.

HEIDEGGER, 1933 Heidegger became rector of Freiburg University in May 1933, the year Hitler came to power. Heidegger's rectoral address, "The Self-Assertion of the German University," has certain applications to 2006. Celan visited Heidegger at Todtnauberg, Heidegger's mountain cabin, in 1967. See John Felstiner, *Paul Celan: Poet, Survivor, Jew* (New Haven: Yale UP, 1995), pp. 245–247. To use Heidegger's language, the "Black Forest" was not "salutary." The guest kept household, not the host. In Richard Crashaw's "Prayer:" *... the heart, / That studies this high art, / Must be a sure house-keeper.*

COMPASS This poem has been carved as a continuous text around the perimeter of a circular stone by Nova Scotian stonemason Heather Lawson. The stone is set at the centre of a maze on the grounds of the Nova Scotia Agricultural College in Truro.

AIKEN DRUM The source of this poem's title is given in the note on the epigraphs. The traditional Scottish nursery rhyme cited is polyphonic with possible meaning, although as far as I know it has never been suggested that Aiken Drum and Willy Wood enact a ritual pattern of immortality and mortality, or that in alchemical language Aiken Drum is mercury, Willy Wood the sacrificial king. At another level, the pair are twins, the dioscuri, the lords of limit. The Scottish poem's locating Aiken Drum's house in the moon recalls, for me, Dante's journey. The moon is the first of the planetary spheres he reaches after leaving the Earthly Paradise on the summit of the Mount of Purgatory. The moon of the *Paradiso* is occupied by those who have paid less than they vowed. In the medieval scholastic scheme, the moon also corresponds to grammar. It reflects a certain splendour.

MEDICINE BUNDLE The poem is based upon a chapter in John Douglas Leechman's *Indian Summer* (Toronto: Ryerson Press, 1949). Leechman is the anthropologist who purchases the bundles. He was the first Director of Western Canadiana at the Glenbow Foundation in Calgary.

BOOKWORK This poem was commissioned by Gaspereau Press to celebrate its removal to new quarters. It was published by the Press as a hand-set broadsheet on September 9, 2004. Heidelberg is a respected manufacturer of printing presses.

A SENSIBLE HORIZON The poem is based upon Bishop's family associations in Nova Scotia, her affection for the province and the wish she expressed to her cousin, Phyllis Sutherland of The Falls, Colchester County, that she, Bishop, should be buried in an abandoned cemetery on the Waugh River, near Tatamagouche, Nova Scotia. One of Bishop's friends has told me that Bishop used to practise *Sortes Bowditchianae*, the chance selection of advisory texts or divinations (as in *Sortes Virgilianae* or *Sortes Biblicae*), using the evolutions at sea section of Nathaniel Bowditch's *The New American Practical Navigator* (there are many editions, but my copy, from which the epigraph is taken, is dated 1844).

ABATOS Abatos was the name of one of the four horses pulling Pluto's chariot.

AFTER MONTEVERDI The poem draws upon Monteverdi's opera *Orfeo*, as well as Rilke's *Sonnets to Orpheus* and Cocteau's film *Orphée*.

TO CLYTIE Thomas Moore is the poet quoted in the first eight lines. The italicized words come from his song "Believe me, if all those endearing young charms." In the nineteenth century it was common to have a marble or bisque bust of Clytie sitting on top of the parlour piano in allusion to Moore's song and his collection *Irish Melodies* (1807–1834).

THE FAITHFUL HUNTRESS
Ramsay's *Victoria Kynaston* (1749) is
in the Beaverbrook Art Gallery
in Fredericton, New Brunswick.
This poem is part of a con-
versation with Anne Comp-
ton, whose remarkable poem
"Victoria's Recitative," published
in *Processional* (Markham, Ontario:
Fitzhenry & Whiteside, 2005),
was its inception. Her book con-
tains a reproduction of the paint-
ing. My poem is also indebted
to Sacheverell Sitwell's *Conversation
Pieces: A Survey of English Domestic Portraits
and Their Painters* (London: Batsford,
1936). A letter by Jane Austen is
quoted in the poem's final stanza.
See Henry Austen, "Biographi-
cal Notice of the Author," in *The
Novels of Jane Austen*, edited by R. W.
Chapman (Oxford: Clarendon,
1933), Vol. 5, p. 8. The Renais-
sance art of rhetorical hand
gestures alluded to in stanza four,
an art still alive for Ramsay and
other painters of the Enlighten-
ment, is discussed and illustrated
in B. L. Joseph's *Elizabethan Acting*
(London: Oxford UP, 1951).

FLAUGHT The remarks quoted
in stanza four are those of the
American modern-art histo-
rian, critic and journalist John
Canaday, who applies them to
Giorgione. See his *The Lives of the
Painters* (New York: Norton &
Co., 1969), vol. 1, p. 183.

WIND CHIMES The poem cel-
ebrates the marriage of Elizabeth
and Jamie Paterson.

SEPTEMBER AIR The poem cel-
ebrates the marriage of Kim and
Mark Cameron.

CHINESE PLATE In the last
stanza, the "lute's thirteen/studs"
are standard in number and serve
roughly as the equivalents of frets
on a guitar's neck.

THREE FRIENDS OF SUMMER
The "three friends," plum, pine
and bamboo, are a constant motif
in Japanese Imari ceramics. In
this poem, they bear an analo-
gous relationship to the triadic
structure of Taoism.

RULES FOR THE TONES OF A
LUTE The poem's last line refers
to a step which carries no weight
in a Tai Chi set.

ELEGY FOR THE GREAT AUKS
The last line begins in an entry
in one of Kafka's notebooks. See
Franz Kafka, *The Blue Octavo Notebooks*,
translated by E. Kaiser and E.
Wilkins (Cambridge, MA: Exact
Change, 1991), p. 12. Some other
lines derive from F. A. Lucas, *The
Expedition to the Funk Island, with Observa-
tions Upon the History and Anatomy of the
Great Auk* (Washington: Smithson-
ian Institution, 1890).

SABLE The poem was written as
response to the Sable Island pho-
tographs of Thaddeus Holownia.
The sparrow in the poem is the
Ipswich Sparrow, which breeds
only on Sable Island.

THE MYSTERIOUS BARRICADES
The title's reference is to Cou-
perin's harpsichord piece, "Les
Barricades Mystérieuses."

WITTGENSTEIN'S CIRCLE See
Norman Malcolm, *Ludwig Wittgen-
stein: A Memoir* (Oxford: Oxford UP,
1984), pp. 44–45.

THE SHARDS See Gershom
Scholem, *On the Kabbalah and Its
Symbolism* (New York: Schocken,
1969), pp. 110, 112–115.

MOZART'S STARLING The con-
certo used in "Mozart's Starling"
is K453, written in 1784. Alfred
Einstein links the concerto's
finale to *Die Zauberflöte*, which
was written and performed in
1791, the year of Mozart's death.
Mozart's beloved starling died
in 1787. Edward Holmes's *The Life
of Mozart* (London, 1845), several
times re-edited and reprinted,
contains an empathetic account.

CATCHING BREATH: "ABATOS"
& OTHERS The sentence "A
fool's fool is the king" is a para-
phrased translation of words spo-
ken by another Alias-Moon, the
hero of Diderot's novel *Le Neveu de
Rameau*, written in 1762, although
not published until 1823. The
quotations from Dostoevsky's
Notes from Underground are taken from
Ralph Matlaw's translation
(New York: E. P. Dutton & Co.,
1960). Words of Mandelstam
appear in the essay's final para-
graph. And now, to quote from
the last poem by Zen nun Ryo-
nen, "I have said enough about
moonlight."

ACKNOWLEDGEMENTS

Earlier versions of some poems in this collection
were published in *The Antigonish Review, The Dalhousie Review,*
the Newsletter of the Elizabeth Bishop Society of
Nova Scotia and in a chapbook entitled *After Monteverdi*
(Sackville, NB: Harrier Editions, 1997). Without the
encouragement of the late George Sanderson, editor of
The Antigonish Review, a few of the poems would not have
gone beyond notebook drafts. I am deeply grateful
to Amanda Jernigan for editing the poems and aptly
seeing where changes should be made. I also thank
Thaddeus Holownia and Douglas Lochhead. This book
is dedicated to my wife, the first friend of summer.

A NOTE ON THE TYPE

This book uses two typefaces. The roman type is Bembo, one of the best loved and most familiar book types of the twentieth century. First issued by the Monotype Corporation in 1929, Bembo is based on types cut at Venice in 1495 by Francesco Griffo for the great humanist publisher Aldus Manutius. Monotype named its revival after Pietro Bembo, the author in whose book these letterforms were rediscovered. ⸿ In 1499, four years after Griffo cut the types that were the basis for Bembo, Aldus Manutius commissioned Griffo to cut the first italic type. In the beginning, italic types were designed and used independent of roman types; it was not until the seventeenth century that the typesetters of the Baroque period began the now common practice of mixing roman and italic on the same line. Perhaps this is why when the Monotype Corporation went looking for an italic to pair with Bembo's roman in 1929, they ignored Griffo's fine italics and considered later italics as models. The italic Monotype matched with Bembo was based on the work of the writing master Ludovico degli Arrighi, dating to 1526; it is in many ways a softer rendering of an italic Monotype issued in 1923 named Blado. The italic used in this book is yet another design, Fairbank, which was initially considered as a companion for Bembo, but then rejected. Fairbank was designed by the English calligrapher Alfred Fairbank for the Monotype corporation in 1928. ⸿ Both digital types have been somewhat modified from their factory-issued state in an effort to honour the spirit of the original designs. – A S

Gaspereau Press acknowledges the support of the
Canada Council for the Arts, the Nova Scotia Department of
Tourism, Culture & Heritage and the Government of Canada
through the Book Publishing Industry Development Program.

Typeset in Bembo & Fairbank by Andrew Steeves & printed offset
at Gaspereau Press. The title page engraving was hand-printed
from the original wood block in each copy of the book.

1   3   5   7   6   4   2

Library and Archives Canada Cataloguing in Publication

Sanger, Peter, 1943–
Aiken Drum / Peter Sanger.
Poems.
Includes bibliographical references.
ISBN 1-55447-015-3 (bound)   ISBN 1-55447-014-5 (pbk.)
I. Title. PS8587.A372A65 2006   C811'.54   C2005-907348-9

GASPEREAU PRESS LIMITED
Gary Dunfield & Andrew Steeves
PRINTERS & PUBLISHERS
47 CHURCH AVENUE, KENTVILLE, NOVA SCOTIA
CANADA B4N 2M7   WWW.GASPEREAU.COM